HORSES SET I

SHETLAND PONIES

BreAnn Rumsch
ABDO Publishing Company

Published by ABDO Publishing Company, 8000 West 78th Street, Edina, Minnesota 55439. Copyright © 2011 by Abdo Consulting Group, Inc. International copyrights reserved in all countries. No part of this book may be reproduced in any form without written permission from the publisher. The Checkerboard Library™ is a trademark and logo of ABDO Publishing Company.

Printed in the United States of America, North Mankato, Minnesota.
042010
092010

 PRINTED ON RECYCLED PAPER

Cover Photo: Alamy
Interior Photos: Alamy pp. 5, 11, 13, 15, 17, 19, 21; iStockphoto p. 6; Peter Arnold p. 9; Photolibrary p. 7

Editor: Megan M. Gunderson
Art Direction & Cover Design: Neil Klinepier

Library of Congress Cataloging-in-Publication Data

Rumsch, BreAnn, 1981-
  Shetland ponies / BreAnn Rumsch.
      p. cm. -- (Horses)
  Includes index.
  ISBN 978-1-61613-422-8
  1. Shetland pony--Juvenile literature. I. Title.
  SF315.2.S5R86 2011
  636.1'6--dc22
                              2010010032

CONTENTS

WHERE SHETLANDS CAME FROM

Throughout time, people have depended on horses of every shape and size. These powerful mammals all belong to the family **Equidae**. Scientists can trace horses back about 60 million years. Their earliest ancestor was eohippus. This small creature was about the size of a fox.

The Shetland pony is one of today's smallest horse **breeds**. It originated in Scotland's Shetland Islands, where it served as a workhorse. Scotsmen used the ponies to haul **peat** for their fires.

In 1885, Shetland ponies arrived in North America. Within 50 years, a second Shetland pony breed emerged there. Today, that breed is known

as the American Shetland pony. Though different, both Scottish and American Shetlands are popular with horse lovers.

Shetland ponies are built for life on the rugged hills of the Shetland Islands.

WHAT SHETLANDS LOOK LIKE

The Scottish Shetland pony's features developed from its original surroundings. The Shetland Islands have harsh winter weather. So, the pony's bushy mane and tail help block the wind. In winter, a double coat provides extra warmth. The pony **sheds** this thick hair in summer to reveal a smooth, shiny coat.

The Scottish Shetland pony has powerful shoulders and a short, wide back. Its legs are short and strong. The pony's small head features a broad forehead and **muzzle**.

The Scottish Shetland has small ears, large nostrils, and sturdy jaws.

The American Shetland has an elegant appearance.

On average, Scottish Shetlands weigh about 400 pounds (180 kg). They average 40 inches (102 cm) tall. This height is measured from the ground to the pony's **withers**.

The American Shetland looks more graceful than the Scottish Shetland. Its legs are long and fine, and it stands about 46 inches (117 cm) tall. This **breed** has a smooth coat, yet it retains the thick Scottish mane and tail.

What Makes Shetlands Special

Scottish Shetland ponies are known for their small size and great strength. For their size, they are one of the strongest horse **breeds**. These ponies can pull between two and five times their own body weight!

With such power, these small ponies once worked in coal mines. In the 1840s, miners used strong Scottish Shetland ponies to haul coal through tight tunnels.

Today, Shetlands make up for their small size with their big personalities! Some people think

Shetlands are stubborn and strong willed. Yet they are actually bright, happy animals. When well trained, these ponies are easy to manage and eager to please.

Strong, gentle Shetlands make perfect ponies for children.

COLOR

Shetland ponies come in many colors! Common colors are bay, chestnut, black, gray, and dun. In addition, Scottish Shetlands are often **dappled**. Blue roan or **pinto** coats are also common.

A bay pony has a light to dark reddish brown coat. Its points are black. Points are the pony's legs, mane, and tail. A pony with a brown coat and the same color or lighter points is a chestnut.

Black ponies have all black hairs unless they have markings. Markings are solid white patches on the head and the legs.

A pony with white hairs on dark skin is a gray. A dun pony displays a light yellow to dark tan coat. Its points are black or another dark color. A blue roan pony has black hairs mixed with white hairs.

With regular grooming, your Shetland's coat will stay clean and healthy. Use a rubber currycomb and a body brush to remove dirt and dust. Then use a comb to help untangle your pony's thick mane and tail.

With so many coat colors to choose from, Shetland ponies offer owners much variety.

CARE

Scottish Shetland ponies are happiest outside, where they can roam freely. Even so, they still need shelter. In a **pasture**, trees or tall bushes can block harsh wind. An open shed offers cover from rain or snow.

All Shetland ponies need indoor shelter, too. Owners should provide their pony with its own stable stall. This space should have plenty of fresh air and clean bedding.

Sometimes, Shetland ponies need special care from a veterinarian. This doctor can help prevent sickness by **deworming** the pony and giving it **vaccines**. He or she can also float the pony's teeth. Filing down the teeth keeps them even and prevents chewing problems.

Your pony's hooves need frequent care. You should clean them with a hoof pick every day. Sometimes a farrier will need to visit. He or she will trim your pony's hooves and replace its horseshoes.

In cold climates, a horse blanket can provide extra warmth for your Shetland.

FEEDING

On the Shetland Islands, food can be hard to find. Long ago, Shetland ponies adapted to grazing on rough grasses there. They also ate seaweed that washed up on shore! Today, Scottish Shetlands are still happiest when grazing.

Before a pony grazes, owners should remove all harmful plants from the **pasture**. If it's hungry enough, a pony may eat dangerous thistle or nightshade. The pasture should also be free of garbage and broken fences. Fresh, clean water must always be available.

Scottish Shetlands eat fewer grains and lush grasses than other horse **breeds**. Grains include oats and bran. The rest of their diet consists of hay, such as dried timothy grass.

Apples and carrots make fun, tasty treats for Shetlands!

Shetland ponies need less food than larger horse **breeds**. The total amount of food they need depends on several factors. These include age, size, and work level.

THINGS SHETLANDS NEED

Shetlands make great riding ponies. They also make wonderful ponies for driving carts. These jobs each require different equipment called tack. No matter what kind of tack your Shetland needs, make sure it fits comfortably.

A riding pony's tack includes a saddle and a bridle. The saddle keeps the rider's weight from harming the pony's back. Stirrups attach to the saddle. The rider places his or her feet in them while riding.

The bridle includes a headstall that fits over the pony's head. A metal bit goes in the pony's mouth and attaches to reins. The rider uses the reins to direct the pony.

A cart pony's tack includes a bridle and a harness. A harness's many parts connect the pony to its load. Reins help the driver tell the pony where to travel.

Owners should clean their pony's tack after every use. This helps it last longer. Cleaning tack also protects the pony from germs.

How Shetlands Grow

Like all horses, an adult female Shetland is called a mare. She mates with an adult male called a stallion. Then, the mare may become **pregnant**. After about 11 months, she gives birth to a baby pony.

A baby pony is called a foal. After the foal is born, its mother licks it clean. Within an hour, the wobbly foal learns to stand.

The newborn foal must quickly learn to nurse. For only a short time, the mare's milk has colostrum in it. Colostrum helps protect the foal from harmful diseases.

The Shetland Pony Stud-Book Society keeps records of Scottish Shetland breeding.

After about six months, the foal is **weaned**. It will continue growing alongside other young horses. Most horses live 20 to 30 years. Healthy ponies generally live longer than larger horses.

TRAINING

The best time to begin training any pony is when it is young. A young foal most easily learns to let people touch it. After this lesson, it begins wearing a halter on its head. This tack makes the pony easier to handle. Soon, the pony learns to lead on a rope. This is similar to how a dog walks on a leash.

Shetland ponies are quick learners. They may become bored with long, repetitive training. So, trainers give short lessons and teach ponies new skills one at a time.

Shetlands are athletic animals. Once they have completed basic training, they can be trained for driving a cart or riding. Many Shetlands also train for driving and jumping competitions. These **versatile** ponies offer horse lovers many fun options in a small package!

Riding a Shetland pony can be an exciting adventure!

GLOSSARY

breed - a group of animals sharing the same ancestors and appearance. A breeder is a person who raises animals. Raising animals is often called breeding them.

dappled - marked with small spots of a different color or shade from the background.

deworm - to rid of worms.

Equidae (EEK-wuh-dee) - the scientific name for the family of mammals that includes horses, zebras, and donkeys.

muzzle - an animal's nose and jaws.

pasture - land used for grazing.

peat - a piece of heavy turf cut and dried for use as fuel.

pinto - marked with patches of white and another color.

pregnant - having one or more babies growing within the body.

shed - to cast off hair, feathers, skin, or other coverings or parts by a natural process.

vaccine (vak-SEEN) - a shot given to prevent illness or disease.

versatile - having many uses.

wean - to accustom an animal to eating food other than its mother's milk.

withers - the highest part of a horse's or other animal's back.

WEB SITES

To learn more about Shetland ponies, visit ABDO Publishing Company on the World Wide Web at **www.abdopublishing.com**. Web sites about Shetlands are featured on our Book Links page. These links are routinely monitored and updated to provide the most current information available.

INDEX